Longman Test Practice Kits

Mathematics

Key Stage 2

Brian Speed • *Linda Terry*

Longman

Series editors

Geoff Black and Stuart Wall

Titles available

Key Stage 2

English

Mathematics

Science

Key Stage 3

English

Mathematics

Science

Addison Wesley Longman Ltd

Edinburgh Gate,

Harlow,

CM20 2JE

England

and Associated Companies throughout the world

First published 1998

Third impression 1998

ISBN 0582 31574-3

British Library Cataloguing-in-Publication Data
A catalogue record for this book is available from the British Library.

Set by 32 in 13/19pt Frutiger light
Printed in Great Britain by Henry Ling Ltd.
at the Dorset Press, Dorchester, Dorset

Table of contents

The Key Stage 2 National Tests

How they work

During the Years 3–6 your child will be studying Mathematics, Science and English as part of Key Stage 2 of the National Curriculum. At the end of Year 6 (at age 11) your child will take the National Curriculum Tests in each of these subjects.

These written National Tests (sometimes called SATs) will take place in May of Year 6. The Tests are taken in your child's own school, but they will be marked by examiners from outside the school.

There will be two written exam papers for Mathematics, one to be taken without a calculator, and the other with a calculator available. Each exam lasts about 45 minutes. There will also be a mental arithmetic test which lasts about 15 minutes.

The results of the National Test will be given by the end of July, together with the results of the classroom assessments made by your child's teacher. Your child's results will be expressed as a Level for each of these assessments: one for the National Test and one for the teacher assessment.

You will also receive a summary of the Key Stage 2 results achieved by all the other students in your child's school, and for all students nationally. You will then be able to check your child's progress against that of other students of their age.

Levels of achievement

At Key Stage 2, each subject is divided into Levels: from Level 2 to Level 6. The table below illustrates what percentage of students, nationally, are expected to gain each Level. You can see from the table that the average student is expected to reach Level 4 by the end of Key Stage 2.

Percentages of students reaching a particular Level in Mathematics

Level	Percentage
1	0
2	12
3	38
4	39
5	10
6	1

This book concentrates on Levels 3–5 and presents questions of the type your child can expect to face in the actual examination. The Level of the work is shown next to each topic heading or subheading.

When your child tries the Test practice papers, please remember that you should *not* let them use a calculator for the *non*-calculator paper.

Using this book

Mathematics at Key Stage 2

The National Curriculum divides Mathematics at Key Stage 2 into four sections called Attainment Targets (ATs).

AT1   Using and Applying Mathematics
AT2   Number
AT3   Shape, Space and Measures
AT4   Handling Data

AT1, Using and Applying Mathematics, is assessed by your child's teacher in the classroom. It is the other three ATs (AT2, AT3 and AT4) that are examined in the National Tests.

Part 1 Self-check revision

Part 1 (pages 4–56) of this book provides a brief outline of what your child needs to know under each of the topic headings examined in the National Tests for Mathematics. Work through the revision topics in Part 1 with your child *before* you try the actual tests in Part 2; add a tick to the Revision Progress chart on page 4 to show that a topic has been revised. To make the revision more active and interesting, you will find fill-in blanks within the topics to help you check that your child understands the topic and can work through the examples. Answers to all the blank spaces can be found at the end of Part 1 (page 55).

Part 2 Test practice papers

- **Questions**   Three Test practice papers, one without a calculator, one with a calculator and a mental arithmetic test.
- **Answers and Mark scheme**   Solutions to all the questions, with breakdown of marks awarded.

The questions will test your child's ability as regards the four main skills:

- Knowledge and understanding
- Handling information
- Interpretation and evaluation
- Problem solving

PART 1

Self-check revision

In this part of the book you will find a brief, easy-to-use review of the topics and techniques that your child is expected to know for their National Test in Mathematics. The ten topics selected cover the three Attainment Targets (ATs) outlined on page 3 as being the focus of the National Test. To encourage your child to make their revision more active and interesting, work through the self-check revision questions in each topic chapter. These questions take the form of blank spaces to be filled in by your child. You can then assess your child's ability by checking their answers against those provided at the end of Part 1 on pages 55–56.

After your child has revised a topic and completed the questions set on that topic, place a tick in the appropriate box in the Revision Progress Chart below. This will help you to keep a record of your child's progress. It will be best if your child revises all ten topics *before* you suggest that they attempt the Test practice papers in Part 2 of the book.

Revision progress chart

	topic	tick when revised
1	**Number**	
1.1	Place value	
1.2	Multiplying by 10, 100, 1000	
1.3	Dividing by 10 or 100	
1.4	Approximations	
1.5	Rounding decimals	
1.6	Addition	
1.7	Subtraction	
1.8	Multiplication	
1.9	Division	
1.10	Inverse operations	
2	**Number pattern**	
2.1	Special numbers	
2.2	Number sequences	
2.3	Negative numbers	
2.4	Calculations with negative numbers	

3	**Fractions and percentages**	
3.1	Fractions	
3.2	Equivalent fractions	
3.3	Addition of fractions	
3.4	Finding a fraction of an amount	
3.5	Percentage	
3.6	Finding a percentage of	
4	**Symmetry**	
4.1	Reflective symmetry	
4.2	Lines of symmetry	
4.3	Rotational symmetry	
4.4	Shapes with both types of symmetry	
5	**Co-ordinates**	
6	**Shapes**	
6.1	2D shapes	
6.2	Triangles	
6.3	Quadrilaterals	
6.4	Congruency	
6.5	Transformations	
6.6	3D shapes	
6.7	Nets	
6.8	Angles	
6.9	Perimeter	
6.10	Area	
6.11	Volume	
7	**Measures**	
7.1	Length	
7.2	Converting metric units of length	
7.3	Capacity	
7.4	Weight	
7.5	Metric measure	
7.6	Time	

8	**Data handling**	
8.1	Lists and tables	
8.2	Graphs and charts	
8.3	Data	
8.4	Pie charts	
9	**Averages**	
9.1	The mode	
9.2	The median	
9.3	The mean	
9.4	The range	
10	**Probability**	
10.1	Likely or unlikely?	
10.2	Probability fractions	

Number

1.1 Place value LEVEL 3

The **digits** 0 1 2 3 4 5 6 7 8 9 are used to make numbers.
The position of the digit in the number shows its value.
For example, look at the value of each digit **6** below:

6̲72   16̲3   146̲

means 6 hundreds   means 6 a_____   means 6 units

Ordering is placing numbers in order of size.
This is done by looking at the position of the digits which make up the number.
For example, suppose you need to order these numbers, lowest first:

396   274   359   816

First, you should select the lowest digit in the hundreds (2̲74), and then select the next lowest digit in the hundreds. Here we find that we have two numbers that are equal **b**_____ (3̲96 and 3̲59) so we have to select the number which has the smallest ten (35̲9). As 39̲6 is the next lowest number, this leaves only 816 as the largest number, since it has the highest digit in the hundreds place. So the correct order is:

274   359   396   816

Each **column** of place value varies by a value of 10:

millions, hundreds of thousands, tens of thousands, thousands, hundreds, tens, and units.

The columns are grouped together in three's separated by a small space (sometimes this will be a comma):

1 000 000 or 1,000,000 (one million)
10 000 or 10,000 (ten thousand)
but 100 (one hundred, not 1,00)

Answers can be found on page 55

1.2 Multiplying by 10, 100, 1000 LEVEL 4

← moving a digit one place to the left means that it becomes 10 times bigger.

→ moving a digit one place to the right means that it becomes 10 times smaller.

If a number is multiplied by 10, it means that all the digits move **one** place to the left, and a 0 is placed on the **c**_____ hand side of the number. For example:

$5 \times 10 = 50$

$32 \times 10 = 320$

$18 \times 10 = 180$

If a number is multiplied by 100, it means that all the digits move **two** places to the left, and 00 is placed on the right-hand side of the number. For example:

$9 \times 100 = 900$

$67 \times 100 = 6700$

$33 \times 100 = 3300$

If a number is multiplied by 1000, it means that all the digits move **three** places to the left, and **d**_____ is placed on the right-hand side of the number.

1.3 Dividing by 10 or 100 LEVEL 4

If a number is divided by 10 it means that all the digits move **one** place to the right.

This makes it look as if one 0 has been taken away. For example:

$50 \div 10 = 5$

$700 \div 10 = 70$

$860 \div 10 = $ **e**_____

Answers can be found on page 55

If a number is divided by 100 it means that all the digits move **two** places to the right. This makes it look as if 00 has been taken away. For example:

$300 \div 100 = 3$

$8800 \div 100 =$ **f** _____

But $860 \div 100 = 8.6$, which involves the use of the decimal point.

1.4 Approximations LEVEL 3

Approximations are used when an answer which is 'near enough' or 'close to' is good enough for us to use. This is called **rounding off**. $\approx$ and $\simeq$ are symbols which are used to mean 'approximately equal to'. It is possible to approximate to the nearest 10, the nearest 100, etc.

To round off a number we have to look at the end digits.

Rounding to the nearest 10
To round to the nearest 10, we either round *down* to the ten below, or round *up* to the ten above. To see if we round up or round down, just look at the **unit** digit:

1 2 3 or 4   we round DOWN
5 6 7 8 or 9   we round UP
0   we don't have to round off at all.

For example:

32   would round down to 30 (because of the 2)
47   would round up to 50 (because of the 7)
285   would round up to 290 (because of the 5)
761   would round **g** _____

Rounding to the nearest 100
We either round down to the hundred below or round up to the hundred above. To see if we round up or round down, just look at the **tens** digit.

0 1 2 3 or 4   we round DOWN
5 6 7 8 or 9   we round UP

Answers can be found on page 55

When rounding off to the nearest 100 we ignore the units digit. For example:

256   would round up to 300 (because of the 5)
2708   would round down to 2700 (because of the 0)
324   would round **h**_____

Rounding to the nearest 1000

We either round down to the thousand below or round up to the thousand above. To see if we round up or round down, just look at the **hundreds** digit.

0 1 2 3 or 4   we round DOWN
5 6 7 8 or 9   we round UP

When rounding off to the nearest 1000 we ignore the tens and the units digits. For example:

6894   would round up to 7000 (because of the 8)
3182   would round down to 3000 (because of the 1)
8509   would round **i**_____

1.5 Rounding decimals LEVEL 5

Rounding to the nearest whole number

We either round down to the whole number below or round up to the whole number above. To see if we round up or round down, just look at the **first decimal place** digit.

0 1 2 3 or 4   we round DOWN
5 6 7 8 or 9   we round UP

When rounding off to the nearest whole number we ignore all the digits after the first decimal place. For example:

4.8   would round up to 5 (because of the 8)
7.08   would round down to 7 (because of the 0)
3.5   would round **j**_____

Answers can be found on page 55

Rounding to 1 decimal place

We either round down or we round up to give a number with one decimal place. To see if we round up or round down, just look at the **second decimal place** digit.

    0 1 2 3 or 4   we round DOWN

    5 6 7 8 or 9   we round UP

When rounding off to 1 decimal place we ignore all the digits after the second decimal place. For example:

    5.29   would round up to 5.3 (because of the 9)

  15.928   would round down to 15.9 (because of the 2)

    4.67   would round **k** _____

1.6 Addition LEVEL 3

There are many ways of saying 'add':

    total   sum of   plus   put together

Addition problems can be arranged like this:

$$23 + 24 = 47 \qquad \text{or} \qquad \begin{array}{r} 23 \\ +\,24 \\ \hline 47 \end{array}$$

Addition of two digit numbers

Two things to remember when adding whole numbers together are:

1 The answer will be larger.

2 Always start by adding the **l** _____ .

If the total of the digits in any column is more than 9, a figure is carried into the next column. (It is important to write down this *carry digit* or you may forget to include it in the addition.) For example:

$$\begin{array}{r} 38 \\ +\,25 \\ \hline 6\,3 \\ \scriptstyle 1 \end{array}$$

Where you put the carry digit (in this case the 1 from $8 + 5 = 13$) doesn't matter, as long as you put it somewhere that you will not forget it for adding in the next column ($3 + 2 + 1 = 6$).

Answers can be found on page 55

Addition of three-digit numbers LEVEL 4

With larger numbers, you still start adding with the units in the right-hand column. For example:

$$
\begin{array}{r}
167 \\
+\ \ 25 \\
\hline
192 \\
{\scriptstyle 1}
\end{array}
\qquad
\begin{array}{r}
2296 \\
+1173 \\
\hline
3469 \\
{\scriptstyle 1}
\end{array}
$$

1.7 Subtraction

There are different ways of saying 'subtract':

   minus   find the difference   take away   less

Subtraction of two-digit numbers

Three things to remember when subtracting two whole numbers are:

1 The larger number must always be written down first.

2 The answer will always be smaller than the larger of the two numbers.

3 Always start with the units.

Subtractions can be set out as:

$$
46 - 13 = 33 \qquad \text{or} \qquad
\begin{array}{r}
46 \\
-13 \\
\hline
33
\end{array}
$$

If you are trying to take a bigger digit from a smaller digit in a column, then you have to remove '10' from the next column to the left and add it to the smaller digit. For example:

$$
\begin{array}{r}
52 \\
-35 \\
\hline
\end{array}
$$

Here we need to take the 5 away from the 2 in the right-hand column, which can't be done. So we look in the left-hand column next to the 2, make the 5 into a 4 and then add the 1 (which has a value of 10) onto the front 2 to make 12. Now we can subtract. Taking 5 from 12 gives 7, taking 3 from 4 gives 1, an answer of 17.

$$
\begin{array}{r}
{\scriptstyle 4}{\scriptstyle 1} \\
\not{5}2 \\
-35 \\
\hline
17
\end{array}
$$

Answers can be found on page 55

Subtractions of numbers with more than 3 digits LEVEL 4

It is important to follow the same rules as above, when solving larger subtraction problems. For example:

$$\begin{array}{r} \overset{6\ 1}{8\cancel{7}4} \\ -\ 215 \\ \hline 659 \end{array} \qquad \begin{array}{r} \overset{2\ 9\ 1}{\cancel{3}\cancel{0}0} \\ -\ 163 \\ \hline 137 \end{array}$$

The example 300 − 163 is tricky as both of the top two right-hand columns are noughts. We first need to take the 3 away from the 0 in the units column, which can't be done. So we look in the left-hand (tens) column next to the 0, make this 10 into a 9 and then add the 1 (which has a value of 10) onto the front of the 0 in the units column to make 10. Of course we now only have 9 instead of 10 in the tens column which means we must adjust the 3 in the hundreds column to 2. Now we can subtract. Taking 3 from 10 gives 7, taking 6 from 9 gives 3, and taking 1 from 2 gives 1, an answer of 137.

1.8 Multiplication LEVEL 3

'Times' by is another way of saying 'multiply by'.
To multiply quickly and accurately it helps to know your tables.
Do learn your tables!
If you are not confident with your tables, then remember that you can find the same answer by multiple addition. For example:

$$3 \times 9 = 9 + 9 + 9 \quad = \boxed{\text{m}}\underline{\hspace{2cm}}$$
$$4 \times 6 = 6 + 6 + 6 + 6 = \boxed{\text{n}}\underline{\hspace{2cm}}$$

Multiplying numbers of more than one digit by one digit LEVEL 4

Two things to remember when multiplying two whole numbers are:

1 The larger number must always be written down first.

2 The answer will always be bigger than the larger number (if we multiply by more than 1).

For example:

$$\begin{array}{r} 213 \\ \times\ \ 4 \\ \hline 85\underset{1}{2} \end{array}$$

Note that your first multiplication of 3 × 4 gives you 12 and we use a carry digit in the same way as we did in addition (see page 11).

Answers can be found on page 55

Long multiplication LEVEL 5

This is where we multiply numbers which are both of more than one digit. When multiplying large numbers you need to use **long multiplication**. Follow through this example:

```
    132
  ×  64
    528
     1
   7920
   1 1
   8448
    1
```

First multiply each of the digits in 132 by the 4 of 64, so 2 × 4, 3 × 4, 1 × 4, to give 528. Then add a 0 in the units column on the next line and multiply 132 by 6, so 2 × 6, 3 × 6, 1 × 6, to give 7 920. You then need to add the two rows (made by multiplying first by the unit digit 4 and then by the tens unit 6) together, to give 8 448.

The most common error in long multiplication is to forget to put the 0 in the row when you are multiplying by the tens digit.

1.9 Division LEVEL 3

'Share by' means the same as divide.
To be able to divide quickly and accurately, it helps to know your tables.
When dividing numbers remember:

1 The answer will always be smaller than the larger of the two numbers (if we divide by more than 1).

2 Division is the only process that you start at the left-hand side.

$$30 \div 10 = 3 \quad \text{or} \quad 10\overline{)30} = 3$$

You can check your answer by repeated subtraction, for example:

$$30 - 10 = 20 \quad \text{1 time}$$
$$20 - 10 = 10 \quad \text{2 times}$$
$$10 - 10 = 0 \quad \text{3 times}$$

Answers can be found on page 55

What if the number will not divide exactly? LEVEL 4

Sometimes the number will not divide exactly, and we may be left with a **remainder**, both within the division itself or after the division.

Follow through these examples:

$$\begin{array}{r} 12 \\ 4\overline{)48} \end{array}$$

This divides exactly. The 4 divides into 4 once, leaving no remainder. The 4 then divides into 8 twice, giving an answer of 12.

$$\begin{array}{r} 1\ 4 \\ 4\overline{)5^16} \end{array}$$

4 divides into 5 once, but leaves remainder 1. This 1 ten is added to the 6 (of 56) to make 16. The 4 then divides into 16 four times exactly. The answer is 14.

$$\begin{array}{r} 1\ 4 \text{ remainder } 3 \\ 4\overline{)5^19} \end{array}$$

Again, 4 divides into 5 once, but leaves remainder 1. This is added to 9 to make 19. The 4 then divides into 19 four times, but leaves a remainder 3. So the answer is 14 remainder 3.

Long Division LEVEL 5

Sometimes you need to be able to divide large numbers. Then you should use **long division**. For example:

352 ÷ 16   means how many 16s in 352

$$\begin{array}{r} 22 \\ 16\overline{)352} \\ 32 \\ 32 \end{array}$$

How many times does 16 go into 3?   Answer 0 remainder 3
How many times does 16 go into 35? Answer 2 remainder 3
How many times does 16 go into 32? Answer 2 exactly.

- Firstly, ask how many times does 16 go into 3? The answer is 0; leave a blank above the 3 in 352.

- So ask how many times does 16 go into 35? The answer is 2 (2 × 16 is 32); put the 2 above the 5 in 352.

- Now multiply the 16 by 2 and write down the answer, 32, under the 35 in 352. Now subtract the 32 from the 35 of 352, giving remainder 3; bring the last 2 (of 352) down and place next to this remainder 3, giving 32.

Answers can be found on page 55

● Then ask how many times does 16 go into 32. The answer is 2 exactly. So the answer to the long division is 22.

You can always *check* your answer by multiplying 22 by 16.

Try some long division yourself with these three problems,

$391 \div 17$ $992 \div 32$ $962 \div 26$

o	p	q

1.10 Inverse Operations LEVEL 5

Sometimes it is useful to understand the relationship between the four operations (or rules), namely addition, subtraction, multiplication and division. This may help you to solve more difficult problems.

$+$ and $-$ can be regarded as a pair of operations

$\times$ and $\div$ can be regarded as a pair of operations

● You can check a subtraction with an addition. For example:

$\begin{array}{r} 261 \\ -129 \\ \hline 132 \end{array}$ It is possible to check this answer by adding 129 and 132. (i.e. add the bottom two numbers and you should get the top number)

● You can check an addition with a subtraction. For example:

$\begin{array}{r} 278 \\ +149 \\ \hline 427 \end{array}$ It is possible to check this answer by subtracting one of the top two lines from the bottom line. This should give you the other number

Answers can be found on page 55

16

Check you can do this by filling in the boxes in these two problems

r
```
    [    ]          62
 −   62        +  48
    48          [    ]
```

s
```
    [    ]         198
 −  198        + 164
   164          [    ]
```

Similarly, it is possible to check the accuracy of multiplying by dividing, and of dividing by multiplying. For example:

```
     36            36      and        243           243
  ×   7        7)252              4)972          ×    4
    252                                            972
```

Check you can do this by filling in the boxes in these two problems

t
```
     43          [    ]
  ×  39       39)1677
   [    ]
```

u
```
   [    ]           26
 26)884          ×  34
                  [    ]
```

Answers can be found on page 55

Number pattern

2.1 Special numbers LEVEL 3

It is important to understand, and to be able to use, certain mathematical words and terms.

Odd numbers

Odd numbers are whole numbers which cannot be divided by 2 exactly.

Odd numbers always end with one of the digits 1, 3, 5, 7 or 9.

The first ten odd numbers are **a** _____

Even numbers

Even numbers are whole numbers which can be divided by 2 exactly.

Even numbers always end with one of the digits 2, 4, 6, 8 or 0.

The first ten even numbers are **b** _____

Square numbers LEVEL 4

Square numbers are numbers that are the answer to a multiplication where a whole number has been multiplied by itself (this is called 'squared'). For example:

16 is a square number because $4 \times 4 = 16$

81 is a square number because **c** _____

The first ten square numbers are **d** _____

A quicker way to write a square number is by writing a small 2 at the top right-hand corner of the number to be squared. The small 2 is called an index (*plural* indices) or power. For example:

3^2 which means 3×3 or 9

Factors

The factors of a number are those numbers which divide exactly into that number. For example:

The factors of 6 are 1, 2, 3 and 6
because each of these numbers divides exactly into 6.

Answers can be found on page 55

The factors of 12 are **e** _____

because each of these numbers divides exactly into 12.

Multiples

The multiples of a number are those numbers that can be divided exactly by that number.

The multiples of 3 are 3, 6, 9, 12, 15, etc.
because 3 will divide exactly into each of them.

The multiples of 5 are **f** _____
because 5 will divide exactly into each of them.

The **lowest common multiple** (LCM) is the smallest number that can be divided exactly by two or more numbers. For example:

To find the LCM of 6 and 9 we list the multiples of each number.

The multiples of 6 are   6, 12, 18, 24, etc.
The multiples of 9 are   9, 18, 27, etc.

We see that 18 is the smallest number that is a multiple of *both* 6 and 9 so we say that 'The LCM of 6 and 9 is 18'

Square roots LEVEL 5

The square root of a number, for example *N*, is that number which when multiplied by itself (squared), equals the number *N*.
Square root has a special sign $\sqrt{}$ which is put in front of the number. For example:

$\sqrt{25}$ means 'the square root of 25'
We know that $5 \times 5 = 25$, so $\sqrt{25} = 5$

Prime numbers

A prime number is a number that has two factors exactly, no more and no less. These two factors are always the number itself and 1.
The first ten prime numbers are 2, 3, 5, 7, 11 and **g** _____

Remember: 1 is *not* a prime number and 2 is the *only* even prime number.

Answers can be found on page 55

Cubic numbers

A cubic number is the answer when a number is multiplied by itself three times. For example:

$1 \times 1 \times 1 = 1$ $2 \times 2 \times 2 = 8$ $5 \times 5 \times 5 = 125$

so 1, 8 and 125 are all cubic numbers

A quick way to write cubic numbers is, like square numbers, to use an index or power; here we place a small 3 in the top right-hand corner of the number. For example:

$4 \times 4 \times 4 = 4^3 = 64$ or $10 \times 10 \times 10 =$ h _____

2.2 Number sequences LEVEL 3

Sometimes there is a **pattern** in a list of numbers. Can you spot the pattern?

2, 4, 6, 8, . . .   these are all i _____ numbers

4, 7, 10, 13, . . . these numbers go up in j _____

2, 4, 8, 16, . . .   these numbers are multiplied by k _____ each time

2.3 Negative numbers LEVEL 3

A number with a minus before it (e.g. -5) is called a **negative number**. Negative numbers are used most often when measuring temperatures.

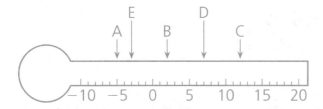

The temperature at A is $-5°C$ at B is l _____   at C is m _____

2.4 Calculations with negative numbers LEVEL 5

We can use the thermometer above to help us to do these calculations.

Answers can be found on page 55

20

We can see on the thermometer that:

from D (7°C) to E (−3°), the temperature has fallen by 10°

from C (12°C) to A (−5°) the temperature has fallen by **n**_____

If the temperature is −6°C and it rises by 11°C, the new temperature will be **o**_____ .

The temperature halfway between -3°C and 7° is **p**_____ .

We can also use a **number line** with positive and negative numbers to do calculations:

Follow through these calculations to see where you start and how you should use the number line to help you calculate.

−6 + 4 means move 4 places to the right from −6 to end up at −2

−6 + 4 = **q**_____

−2 − 3 means move 3 places to the left from −2 to end up at −5

−2 − 3 = **r**_____

6 − 9 means move 9 places to the left from 6 to end up at −3

6 − 9 = **s**_____

Answers can be found on page 55

Fractions and percentages

3.1 Fractions LEVEL 4

A fraction is a part of something. It is less than one whole item.
There are two types of fraction – decimal fractions and vulgar fractions.
(In this section we are dealing with vulgar fractions.)

A **vulgar fraction** is always written like this:

$\dfrac{1}{2}$ means one whole item has been split into 2 equal parts.

The bottom number is called the **denominator**. It tells you how many equal parts the whole item has been split into.

The top number is called the **numerator**. It tells you how many of the equal parts you have.

$\dfrac{2}{3}$ there are two equal parts;
the item has been split into 3 equal parts

3.2 Equivalent fractions LEVEL 5

Equivalent fractions are fractions which are worth the same; they are of equal value. For example:

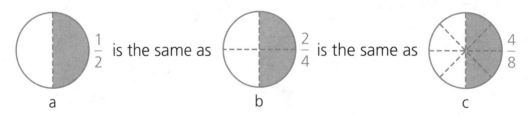

$\dfrac{1}{2}$ is the same as $\dfrac{2}{4}$ is the same as $\dfrac{4}{8}$

a   b   c

It is important to be able to change fractions into equivalent fractions, especially when we have to add or subtract them.

To change any fraction into an equivalent fraction you either divide or multiply both the top and the bottom numbers in the fraction by the *same* number.

Answers can be found on page 55

Dividing top and bottom

$$\frac{9}{12} = \frac{9}{12} \div \frac{3}{3} = \frac{3}{4}$$

We call this **cancelling down**. It is an important part of fraction work.

Multiplying top and bottom

$$\frac{3}{4} = \frac{3 \times 5}{4 \times 5} = \frac{15}{20}$$

$$\frac{2}{5} = \boxed{a} \underline{\hspace{2cm}} = \frac{8}{20}$$

3.3 Addition of fractions

If the fractions have the *same* bottom number (denominator), then you simply add the top numbers and keep the bottom number as it is. For example:

$$\frac{2}{7} + \frac{3}{7} = \frac{5}{7}$$

If the fractions have *different* bottom numbers (denominators) then you need to look at the numbers and find the simplest multipliers to change both fractions into their equivalent fractions. You will then have fractions with the same bottom numbers.

- Sometimes you only need to change *one* fraction. For example:

$$\frac{1}{3} + \frac{5}{12}$$

You need to change the $\frac{1}{3}$ into an equivalent fraction with 12 on the bottom. To do this you can multiply both top and bottom by 4 to give

$$\frac{1 \times 4}{3 \times 4} = \frac{4}{12}$$

You can then rewrite the problem as

$$\frac{4}{12} + \frac{5}{12} = \frac{9}{12}$$

This fraction can then be cancelled down to give

$$\frac{9 \div 3}{12 \div 3} = \frac{3}{4}$$

Answers can be found on page 55

- Sometimes you have to change *both* fractions. For example:

$$\frac{3}{5} + \frac{1}{4}$$

You need to change both fractions into equivalent fractions, with the bottom number being the LCM of 4 and 5. Here the LCM is 20, so

$$\frac{3}{5} + \frac{1}{4} = \frac{3 \times 4}{5 \times 4} + \frac{1 \times 5}{4 \times 5} = \frac{12}{20} + \frac{5}{20} = \frac{17}{20}$$

You may find that sometimes the final answer can be cancelled down. Other times it may give you a top-heavy fraction, that is when the top number is larger than the bottom. If you have a top-heavy fraction, then change the fraction into what is called a **mixed number**.
For example:

$\frac{5}{3}$ is a top-heavy fraction, it will make the mixed number $1\frac{2}{3}$

Now try this yourself.

$$\frac{4}{5} + \frac{5}{6} = \frac{4 \times 6}{5 \times 6} + \frac{5 \times 5}{6 \times 5} = \frac{24}{30} + \frac{25}{30} = \frac{49}{30} = \boxed{b} \underline{\hspace{2cm}}$$

3.4 Finding a fraction of an amount LEVEL 4

Sometimes it is necessary to find a **fractional amount**. For example:

$\frac{1}{2}$ of 8   we recognise that we have to divide 8 by two, to give 4

$\frac{1}{5}$ of 35 we simply divide 35 by 5, to give 7

$\frac{1}{3}$ of 36 will work out to be $\boxed{c}$ \underline{\hspace{3cm}}

If the top number (numerator) of the fraction is more than 1, then we need to find the fraction part as above, but then multiply this by the numerator. For example:

$\frac{2}{3}$ of 15 we divide 15 by 3 to get 5, then we multiply this by 2, to give 10

$\frac{3}{4}$ of 20 will work out to be $\boxed{d}$ \underline{\hspace{2cm}}

Answers can be found on page 55

3.5 Percentage LEVEL 4

Percentage means a fraction out of one hundred.
The sign % is used for percentage.

50% means 50 out of 100

16% means **e** _____

There is a close relationship between percentage and fractions:

36% can be written as $\frac{36}{100}$

27% can be written as **f** _____

Once you have rewritten a percentage as a fraction you may be able to cancel it down.

It is useful to learn the percentages that are used most often as fractions:

$25\% = \frac{1}{4}$ $75\% = \frac{3}{4}$ $50\% = \frac{1}{2}$

$10\% = \frac{1}{10}$ $20\% = \frac{1}{5}$

3.6 Finding a percentage of LEVEL 5

There is a close relationship between fractions and percentages. Sometimes it is easier to turn the percentage part into a fraction. For example, 25% of something is the same as finding $\frac{1}{4}$ of it.

Example

Q Find 20% of £8.

A *If we remember that 20% is the same as $\frac{1}{5}$, then all we have to do is to calculate*

$£8 \div 5 =$ **g** _____

Calculating percentages with your calculator

You should quite easily be able to calculate a percentage by using your calculator. Follow this example to find 35% of £9.80:

Key **35 × 9.8 ÷ 100 =** into your calculator.
You should end up with the answer of £3.43.

Answers can be found on page 55

Problems with percentage

We often have to reduce an amount by a percentage, or increase an amount by a percentage.

Examples

Q Reduce £40 by 5% (maybe in a shop sale).

A We need to calculate 5% of £40, then subtract this from the £40.

5% of £40 is found by

$$\frac{5}{100} \times 40 = \frac{200}{100} = £2$$

Now we need to subtract £2 from the £40 to give £38.

Q Increase £40 by 10%.

A We need to calculate 10% of £40, then add this to £40.
10% of £40 is found by

$$\frac{10 \times 40}{100} = \frac{400}{100} = £4$$

Now we need to add £4 to £40 to give £44.

To change a fraction into a percentage

To change a fraction into a percentage, we change the fraction into an equivalent fraction with a denominator of 100.

Example

Q Hannah had some tests and scored the following results:

English $\frac{16}{20}$ Maths $\frac{7}{10}$ Science $\frac{15}{25}$

Which of the tests gives Hannah her best percentage?

A English $= \dfrac{16 \times 5}{20 \times 5} = \dfrac{80}{100} = 80\%$

Maths $= \dfrac{7 \times 10}{10 \times 10} = \dfrac{70}{100} = 70\%$

Science $= \dfrac{15 \times 4}{25 \times 4} = \dfrac{60}{100} = $ **h** _____

So Hannah's best percentage score is **i** _____ .

Answers can be found on page 55

Symmetry

4.1 Reflective symmetry LEVEL 3

Some shapes can be split in half so that each half looks exactly the same.

If a mirror is placed on the line, it is possible to check whether the shape has been divided properly. If the shape displayed on the other side of the line is the same as if it was a reflection in a normal mirror, we say there is **reflective symmetry**.

4.2 Lines of symmetry LEVEL 4

The line which acts as though it is a mirror creating a reflection is called a **line of symmetry**. It is possible to draw lines of symmetry in more than one way.

Mirror placed across the shape   *Mirror placed down the shape*

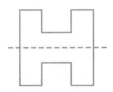   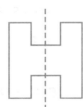

There is only one way of dividing this shape to create a reflection.
There is only **a**_____ line of symmetry.

     This shape has **b**_____ lines of symmetry.

Answers can be found on page 55

4.3 **Rotational symmetry** LEVEL 4

Rotate means to turn. A shape has **rotational symmetry** if it can be turned around the centre of the shape and occupy exactly the same space in at least one other position.

The **order** of rotational symmetry is the number of different positions the shape can occupy, while turning around the centre of the shape, which take up exactly the same space as originally.

This square has rotational symmetry of order 4 because if we rotate the shape around its centre, there are 4 different positions in which the shape occupies the same space, as shown below:

| Start | 1 | 2 | 3 | 4 |

This equilateral triangle has rotational symmetry of order **c** _____ .

This shape has rotational symmetry of order **d** _____ .

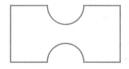

Every shape has an **order of rotational symmetry**. Even a shape that has no other position in which it looks the same, such as this shape of a T, is said to have rotational symmetry of order 1.

However, a shape with rotational symmetry of order 1, is said to have *no* rotational symmetry.

Answers can be found on page 55

4.4 Shapes with rotational and reflective symmetry LEVEL 5

Some shapes have *both* types of symmetry.
For example this letter 'H'

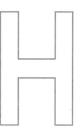

Reflective 2 lines of symmetry	
Rotational of order 2	

This shape has **e**_____ lines of reflective symmetry,
and rotational symmetry of order **f**_____

Answers can be found on page 55

Co-ordinates

This entire topic is at Level 4.

Co-ordinates are two numbers or letters which help to fix the exact position on a grid.

You are describing the position of a point by using numbered lines, called **axes**.

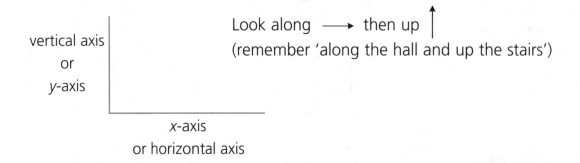

vertical axis
or
y-axis

Look along ⟶ then up ↑
(remember 'along the hall and up the stairs')

x-axis
or horizontal axis

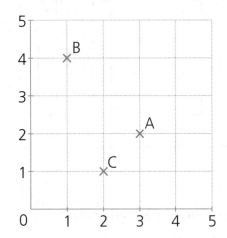

The co-ordinates of *A* are (3, 2)

The co-ordinates of *B* are **a** _____

The co-ordinates of *C* are **b** _____

Answers can be found on page 55

Shapes

6.1 2D shapes LEVEL 3

Two-dimensional (2D) shapes may be sorted into groups depending on their properties. For example:

- The number of lines they have.
- Whether the lines are straight or curved.
- The number of angles (corners).
- The types of angle.

Grouping things is called **classification**.

Circle
1 curved side
no angles

Square
4 straight sides
4 right-angled corners

Rectangle
4 straight sides
4 right-angled corners

Triangle
3 straight sides
3 corners (angles)

Pentagon
5 straight sides
5 angles

Hexagon
6 straight sides
6 angles

Look at this table, and then complete it for the shapes shown above.

Shapes with right angles	Shapes with angles	Shapes with no angles
square	triangle	**d**_____
a_____	pentagon	
	square	
	b_____	
	c_____	

Answers can be found on page 55

6.2 Triangles LEVEL 4

All three-sided shapes are called **triangles.**

There are different types of triangle.

This is an **equilateral** triangle. It has **e** sides of equal length It has 3 equal **f** all 60°	
	This is an **isosceles** triangle It has 2 sides of equal length It has **g** equal angles
This is a **scalene** triangle All its sides are a different length All its angles are different	
	This is a **right-angled** triangle It has one right angle in it

6.3 Quadrilaterals LEVEL 4

All shapes with four sides are called **quadrilaterals**.

All **quadrilaterals** have four angles which add up to 360°

	This is a **square** It has 4 sides of equal length It has 4 right angles
	This is a **rectangle** It has opposite sides of equal length It has 4 right angles

Answers can be found on page 55

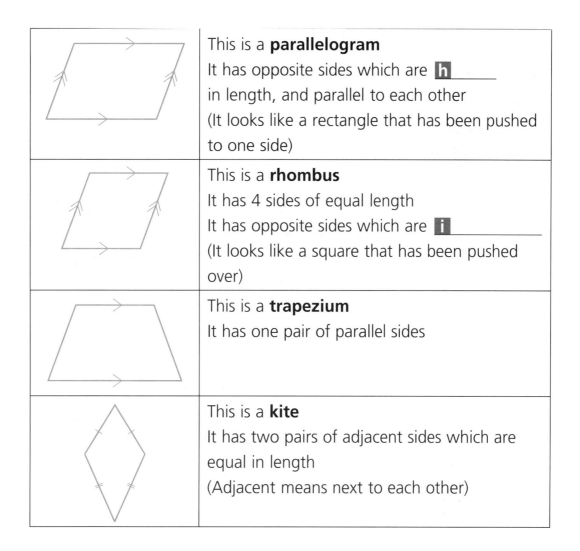

	This is a **parallelogram** It has opposite sides which are **h**_____ in length, and parallel to each other (It looks like a rectangle that has been pushed to one side)
	This is a **rhombus** It has 4 sides of equal length It has opposite sides which are **i**_____ (It looks like a square that has been pushed over)
	This is a **trapezium** It has one pair of parallel sides
	This is a **kite** It has two pairs of adjacent sides which are equal in length (Adjacent means next to each other)

6.4 Congruency LEVEL 4

Shapes that are exactly the same size and shape as each other are said to be **congruent**. For example:

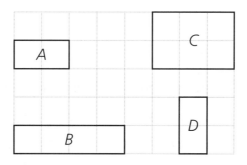

Shape *A* is congruent to which other shape? **j**_____

Answers can be found on page 55

6.5 Transformations LEVEL 4

We can **transform** a shape to an image using any one of the following transformations:

- A **reflection** in a line
- A **rotation** about a point
- A **translation** from one position to another

When we do any of the above transformations then the image and the original shape are **congruent** to each other. For example:

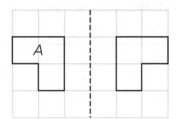

Shape *A* has been reflected in the dotted line.

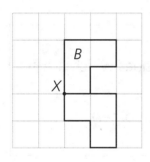

Shape *B* has been **k**_____ about point *X*, through a quarter turn clockwise (90°).

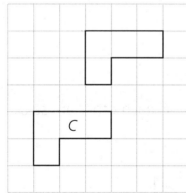

Shape *C* has been **l**_____ 3 squares up and 2 squares to the right.

6.6 3D shapes LEVEL 3

Solid shapes can be sorted into groups depending on their properties.

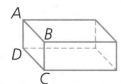

ABCD is a **face** – a flat surface.

AB and *DC* are **edges** – where two surfaces meet.

A is a **vertex**, where three **m**_____ meet.

Note: The plural of *vertex* is *vertices*.

Answers can be found on page 55

Here are some 3D shapes, whose names you should be familiar with.

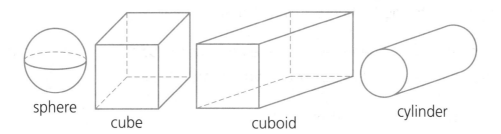

sphere   cube   cuboid   cylinder

The shape with no edges is the **sphere**.

The shape with six equal faces is the **n**_____.

The shapes with no vertices are the **o**_____.

The following shapes all have faces that meet at a point. You should know their names.

 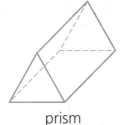 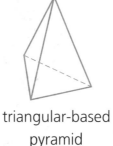 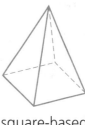

cone   prism   triangular-based pyramid   square-based pyramid

6.7 Nets LEVEL 4

Most of the simple 3D shapes you come across can be made from a **net**. A net is a flat shape that can be cut and folded up to make the solid 3D shape. For example:

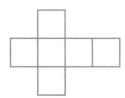

This net will fold to make a **cube**.

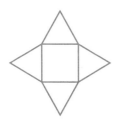

This net will fold to make a **p**_____.

Answers can be found on page 55

6.8 Angles LEVEL 4

Angles are formed when two straight lines meet.

When an angle is measured, it is the amount of **turn** that is measured. Angles are measured in **degrees**, written as °.

To measure angles, use a **protractor** like the one shown here.

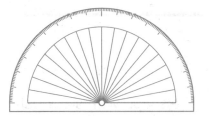

When you measure the size of an angle, make sure the centre of the protractor (labelled O) is placed where the two straight lines meet.

If you face in one direction and then turn once completely round, you have turned through 360°. So,

- half a turn is 180°
- one-quarter of a turn is 90° (this is also known as a right angle), and
- three-quarters of a turn is 270°

Different types of angle LEVEL 5

Angles smaller than 90° are called **acute** angles They are sharp looking If you measure this acute angle it is **q** _____	

Answers can be found on page 55

Angles that are bigger than 90° but smaller than 180° are called **obtuse** angles If you measure this angle it is **r** _____	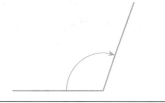
Angles that are bigger than 180° but smaller than 360° are called **reflex** angles. Reflex angles are so wide that they look as if they have been bent backwards If you measure this angle it is **s** _____	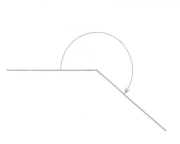

There are certain rules to remember about angles.

The angles inside a triangle all add up to 180°

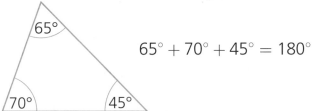

$65° + 70° + 45° = 180°$

For example, to find the size of angle *a* we calculate
$180 - (70 + 35) =$ **t** _____ .

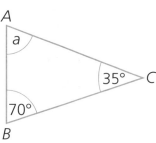

Angles on a straight line add up to 180°

For example, the size of angle *a* is calculated by $180° - 55° = 125°$.

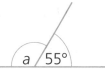

Where two straight lines cross each other they make 4 angles

The two lines **intersect**. Where this happens, opposite angles are the same size as each other.

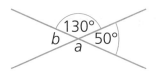

u $a =$ _____

$b =$ _____

Answers can be found on page 55

Where two straight lines run next to each other, without ever crossing, they are parallel (train tracks are like this).

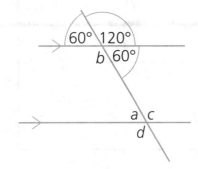

If a line cuts through a pair of parallel lines it is called a **transversal**, and creates many equal angles as seen.

$\boxed{v}$ $a =$ _____ , $b = c = d =$ _____

6.9 Perimeter LEVEL 4

The **perimeter** is the distance around the $\boxed{w}$ _____ of a flat shape.

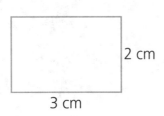

2 cm

3 cm

The perimeter of this rectangle is:
   $3\,\text{cm} + 2\,\text{cm} + 3\,\text{cm} + 2\,\text{cm}$
   $= 10\,\text{cm}$

3 cm

3 cm

The perimeter of this square is:

$\boxed{x}$ _____

6.10 Area LEVEL 4

Area is the amount of space inside a shape. It is measured in square units.

This square is 1 cm by 1 cm – it is one square centimetre, or 1 cm^2.

Six of the square centimetres would fit into this rectangle, so its area is $\boxed{y}$ _____ .

To find the area of any rectangle, you multiply the length by the width.

   $A = l \times w$

Answers can be found on page 55

6.11 **Volume** LEVEL 4

Volume means the amount of space inside a 3D shape. It is measured in cubes.

 This shape is 1 cm by 1 cm by 1 cm
– it is one cubic centimetre or 1 cm^3.

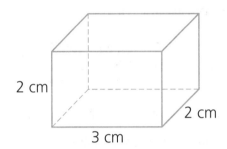

Twelve of the cubic centimetres would fit inside this cuboid, so its volume is

To find the volume of any cuboid, you multiply the length by the width by the height.

   V = l × w × h

Answers can be found on page 55

7 Measures

7.1 Length LEVEL 3

When you measure the **length** of something, it is important to measure accurately. If you use a ruler (or a metre stick or tape measure, etc.) make sure that you start measuring from the beginning of the first unit.

Some rulers have a 'waste end.'

Waste end

Check that you are using your ruler correctly by measuring the length of this line _____ to the nearest millimetre. This line measures **a** _____ mm.

Note: Before you measure something, it is a good idea to estimate (make a sensible guess) about how long the line is. This will help you tell if your answer is sensible.

- To measure smaller lengths, you use **b** _____ . Remember mm is short for millimetres.
- To measure longer lengths, you use **c** _____ . Remember m is short for metres.
- To measure large distances, between towns for example, you use **d** _____ . Remember, km is short for kilometres.

It is important to include the **unit of measurement** whenever you measure anything or write down a distance.

7.2 Converting metric units of length LEVEL 5

Remember the following conversions:

$$10\,mm = 1\,cm$$
$$100\,cm = 1\,m$$
$$1000\,m = 1\,km$$

This line is 3 cm long ————————— it is the same as 30 mm

This line is 45 mm long ————————— it is the same as 4.5 cm

Answers can be found on page 55

Writing a length in a different unit is called converting (or changing) the units. For example:

260 cm converts to **e**_____ m

1275 m converts to **f**_____ km

7.3 Capacity LEVEL 3

Capacity is the amount of liquid in a container. We measure capacity in litres and millilitres.

Capacity is also used to tell us how much a container can hold.

You should be familiar with what a litre is. Do look at your bottles of pop, they are often in either a litre bottle or a 2 litre bottle. If you thought about the following containers, then you should be able to tell that:

A bath holds more than a litre.

A cup holds **g**_____ than a litre.

An oil drum holds **h**_____ than a litre.

A medicine spoon holds **i**_____ than a litre.

Litres and millilitres LEVEL 5

1 litre = 1000 millilitres (ml)

This jug contains lemonade.
It contains 1.5 litres which can be written as
1 litre 500 ml or as 1500 ml.

Questions on capacity can be varied. Here are some situations to work through.

Example 1

Q How much do these two jugs together hold?

A Together these two jugs hold
650 ml + 2.450 litres.
We can add them together as

```
    2 litres 450 ml
  +        650 ml
    ─────────────────
    3 litre  100 ml
    1
```

650 ml   2 litres 450 ml

(Notice that we had a litre to carry because the 450 and 650 made over **j**_____ ml.)

Answers can be found on page 55

Example 2

Q How much liquid is left in the larger jug after the small jug has been filled?

A We subtract the  amount from the larger:

$$
\begin{array}{r}
{}^{1}2 \text{ litres } {}^{1}300 \text{ ml} \\
-\phantom{2 \text{ litres }}900 \text{ ml} \\
\hline
1 \text{ litre } 400 \text{ ml}
\end{array}
$$

This jug holds 900 ml   This jug holds 2.3 litres

(Notice that we had to take 1 litre from the litres and put 1000 ml into the ml column.)

Example 3

Q How much milk is there in 4 full glasses like this?

A We 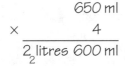 the 650 ml by 4 to get

$$
\begin{array}{r}
650 \text{ ml} \\
\times \phantom{650 \text{ m}} 4 \\
\hline
2_2 \text{ litres } 600 \text{ ml}
\end{array}
$$

This glass holds 650 ml

(Notice that we carried the 2000 ml over into the litres column as 2 litres.)

Example 4

Q How many times can you fill the jug from the bucket?

A We  12 litres by 3 litres, which is 12 ÷ 3 = 4.

This jug holds 3 litres   This bucket holds 12 litres

7.4 Weight LEVEL 3

Weight means heaviness. Sometimes the word **mass** is used.

There is a difference between the two words.

- The **weight** of an object is the amount of pull on that body made by gravity.
- The **mass** of an object is the amount of matter in it.

We measure weight using kilograms (kg) and grams (g).

Answers can be found on page 55

You should be familiar with the weight 1 kilogram, it is the weight of a bag of sugar. You are able to make comparisons like:

Your teacher weighs more than a kilogram.

A bag of crisps weighs **n**_____ than a kilogram.

A bag of potatoes weighs **o**_____ than a kilogram.

This book weighs **p**_____ than a kilogram.

1000 grams = 1 kg LEVEL 5

The weight of this bag can be written as 1200 g, or 1 kg 200 g, or 1.2 kg.

1200 g

7.5 Metric measure LEVEL 5

Today we use **metric** measure for:

- **Length** millimetres, centimetres, metres and kilometres
- **Weight** grams and kilograms
- **Capacity** millilitres and litres

There are many older people who still talk about the old **imperial system** of measures:

- **Length** inches, feet, yards and miles
- **Weight** ounces, pounds and stones
- **Capacity** pints and gallons

This chart will help you to compare metric and imperial measure – you do need to be familiar with them.

	Imperial	*Metric*
length	1 inch	about $2\frac{1}{2}$ cm
	1 foot (12 inches)	about 30 cm
	1 yard (3 feet)	just less than 1 metre
	1 mile	about $1\frac{1}{2}$ km
weight	4 ounces ($\frac{1}{4}$ pound)	about 100 g
	2 pounds	about 1 kg
capacity	2 pints	about 1 litre
	1 gallon	about 4 litres

Answers can be found on page 55

7.6 Time LEVEL 3

Time is often seen on clocks just as it is written down, for example 7.45.

It is important to know whether the time is in the morning or the afternoon, which is why we use:

am to indicate morning

pm to indicate `q`_____

Another way to show morning and afternoon is by using the 24 hour clock, where all the afternoon times run on from 12.00 to 24.00. For example:

3 pm is the same as (3 + 12) which is written as 15.00

7 pm is the same as (7 + 12) which is written as `r`_____

9 am is the same as 9.00

11 am is the same as `s`_____

The questions that you are likely to be asked are about the gap between certain times.

Example

Q   A film started at 4.50 pm and finished at 6.15 pm. How long did it last?

A   You can either do a subtraction or count up time (remember 60 minutes in 1 hour):

$$
\begin{array}{r}
^{5}\,{}^{6} \\
6\,.\,15 \\
-\,4\,.\,50 \\
\hline
1\,.\,25
\end{array}
$$

from 4.50 to 5.00	10 mins
from 5.00 to 6.15	1 hr 15 min
add to give	1 hr 25 min

It doesn't matter which method you use, as long as you can correctly work out the times in situations such as the above.

Answers can be found on page 55

Data handling

8.1 Lists and tables LEVEL 3

Useful information can be presented in the form of a **table**.
Here is a table to show the height of four children.

Name	Height
Joy	1 m 18 cm
Kim	1 m 13 cm
Tom	1 m 21 cm
Vicky	1 m 09 cm

By using the table, you can find out information about the children:

Who is the tallest? **a**_____

Who is the smallest? **b**_____

How much bigger is Joy, than Kim? **c**_____

Sometimes tables show more than one thing. For example, here is a table to show children's preferences at lunchtime.

	Chips	Jacket potato	Baked beans	Cheese flan	Fish fingers	Peas
Joe		✓		✓		✓
Sangita		✓	✓			
Fatima	✓			✓		
Helen		✓	✓		✓	
Sam	✓				✓	✓

By looking at the table you can see that:

Sam had chips, fish fingers and peas.

d_____ had cheese flan and chips.

e_____ children chose baked beans.

Sangita ate **f**_____.

Answers can be found on page 56

45

8.2 Graphs and charts LEVEL 3

A **graph** is a special type of chart or diagram. It shows information clearly, without using a lot of words or figures.

A graph should always have:

1 A title.

2 Labels on the axes, so that you can understand the information.

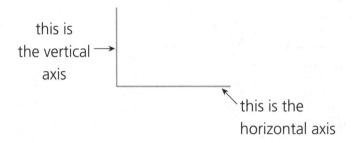

this is
the vertical →
axis

this is the
horizontal axis

Bar chart, or bar graph

A bar chart is a graph where the information is stored in bars or rows.

From this bar chart we can see that:

g_____ children chose blue.

There were **h**_____ children represented in the chart.

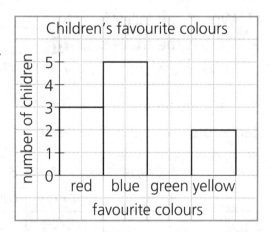

Children's favourite colours

number of children

red   blue   green yellow

favourite colours

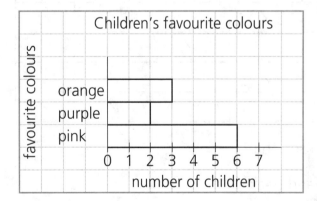

Children's favourite colours

favourite colours

orange
purple
pink

0 1 2 3 4 5 6 7
number of children

A bar chart can also be drawn across the page.

This shows that **i**_____ children chose pink.

Answers can be found on page 56

Pictogram or pictograph

A pictogram is a type of graph which uses pictures to show information. It uses a symbol to represent a certain number of items in the data, this is called the **key**.

From the pictogram we see that:

Eleanor drank **j**_____ glasses.

Altogether there were **k**_____ glasses of squash drunk.

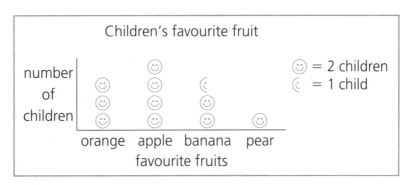

A pictogram to show the glasses of squash drunk at Sharon's party

🥛 = 2 glasses

Mary	🥛 🥛 🥛 🥛 🥛
Nafisa	🥛 🥛 🥛
Sharon	🥛
Eleanor	🥛 🥛 🥛 🥛

Look carefully at this pictogram.

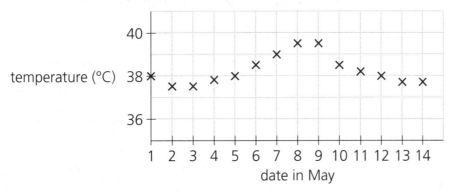

Children's favourite fruit

☺ = 2 children
☾ = 1 child

The key illustrates how we have to split the shape up to illustrate different numbers.

Look at the chart and see that **l**_____ children chose bananas.

Line graph LEVEL 4

A line graph is drawn by plotting points and then joining the points together with a straight line. For example:

You can read information from the graph. For example, in the graph above, we can estimate that Anne's temperature was **m**_____ on 7th May.

Answers can be found on page 56

47

Topic 8

8.3 Data LEVEL 4

'**Data**' is the mathematical word for items of information.
Data is collected by counting the number of items or how often
something happens.

One way of recording data is by using a **tally chart**.
A small line (a tally) is made for each item, and for every fifth entry, a
diagonal line is made through the previous four lines.
For example, we may roll a dice 20 times and keep a record of what
numbers we had.

This information can be collected
in a tally chart as shown.

number of the dice	tally	frequency
1	II	2
2	I	1
3	III	3
4	IIII	5
5	III	3
6	IIII I	6

We have added a **frequency column** on the end of the tally chart, this
also makes the tally chart, a **frequency chart**.
Note that **n**_____ means how often that event has happened.

A **frequency diagram** is like a bar chart, it shows us data about some
situation, and we can get information from it.

Grouped frequency tables
Sometimes there is so much data that it has to be **grouped** into
intervals before it can be shown on a diagram.

Example
A test was marked out of 50.
The results for the whole
school year are given in
the grouped frequency
table opposite.

Test score (interval)	Frequency
0–10	5
11–20	12
21–30	24
31–40	31
41–50	14

Answers can be found on page 56

48

From the table we can see that there were **o**_____ children in this school year.

You could then illustrate this information in a bar chart or a pictogram if you wished.

8.4 Pie Chart LEVEL 5

A pie chart is a circle divided into sectors to show information. Pie charts make it easy to compare amounts since the bigger sectors show the most popular items.

This pie chart shows how six children travel to school.

p_____ children come by car.

1 child comes by **q**_____ .

To find the actual frequencies from a pie chart, it helps to find the proportion of the whole pie chart taken by that section (use fractions or percentages).

This pie chart represents how 100 children used their pocket money.

We see that the number of children who bought sweets was $\frac{1}{2}$ of the 100 children, which was **r**_____ .

The number of children who bought books was **s**_____ .

The percentage of children who saved their money is $\frac{1}{4}$ expressed as a percentage, which is **t**_____ .

Answers can be found on page 56

Averages

Data that has been collected may be used in different ways. Often, we wish to know the **average** figure from our data. There are three different types of average we can use.

9.1 The mode LEVEL 4

The **mode** is the piece of data that occurs the most.
For example, look at this table.

Colour of eyes	Number of children
blue	21
green	3
brown	6

The modal colour (which means the mode colour) is the one that most children in the chart have. This is **a** _____ .

It is possible for there to be more than one mode in a list.
For example, we can see from this table that the modal shoe sizes for the group of children are sizes 4 and 5.

Shoe size	Number of children
3	7
4	9
5	9
6	5

9.2 The median LEVEL 4

The **median** is another word for the middle. If the data is sorted and arranged in order of size (usually starting with the smallest), the median is the middle number in the list. For example, the number of spellings that were correct in a test given to nine pupils were:

4, 2, 9, 6, 5, 8, 2, 9, 7

Arrange the list in order of size: 2, 2, 4, 5, 6, 7, 8, 9, 9

The number in the middle is 6, so the median number of spellings that were correct is **b** _____ .

Answers can be found on page 56

Sometimes there are two numbers in the middle. If this happens, then the median is halfway between the two middle items. For example: The number of correct answers to a table test given to ten pupils were:

4, 5, 5, 7, 7, 8, 8, 8, 9, 9

The two numbers in the middle are 7 and 8, we find halfway between these by adding them together and halving the answer. So here that will be **c**_____ .

Note: If there is an *odd* number of items in our list, there will only be one number in the middle, so the median is that number.

If there is an *even* number of items in the list, there will be two numbers in the middle, and we find the median by **d**_____ them together then halving.

9.3 The mean LEVEL 5

The **mean** is what most people have in mind when they use the word average. To find the mean, you add up all the items of data, then divide by the number of items you had.

Example 1

Q Five children are sitting around a table. They find out that the number of children in each of their families is 2, 1, 4, 2, 2.

Find the mean number of children in their families.

A We add up all the numbers $2 + 1 + 4 + 2 + 2 = 11$.

We then divide by the number of numbers $11 \div 5 = 2.2$.

So, the mean number of children per family is 2.2 children.

Example 2

Q Sophie gained the following scores in her weekly spelling tests:

6, 9, 8, 7, 5

Find her mean score.

A We add all the scores to get **e**_____ .

We then divide by the number of tests to get **f**_____ .

Sophie's mean score is **g**_____ .

Answers can be found on page 56

9.4 The range LEVEL 5

The **range** is the difference between the lowest and the highest number in the data.

For example: from the list 7, 3, 2, 8 and 9, the range will be given by

$$9 - 2 = 7$$

The range is useful when comparing two sets of data.

The smaller the range, the more consistent are the data.

For example, the following table shows the number of points scored in a series of games.

Linda	8	7	8	9	8
David	10	3	4	12	12

Linda's mean score is $(40 \div 5) = 8$ with a range of 2.

David's mean score is $(41 \div 5) = 8.2$ with a range of 9.

You could argue that David is the better player because he has the higher **h**_____ score.

You could also argue that Linda is the better player because, although their mean scores are close, Linda's low range indicates that she is more reliable, she is almost certain to come up with a score of around 8, whereas David will either score well or flop altogether.

In your National Tests (SATs), either answer given above is correct *if* you have given a good reason based on the range and the mean.

Answers can be found on page 56

Probability

10.1 Likely or unlikely? LEVEL 4

Probability is about looking at something and deciding whether the chance of it happening is

    impossible   unlikely   evens   likely   or   certain

For example:

It is **a**_____ that I will meet Queen Victoria.

It is **b**_____ that it will snow in Sheffield in June.

It is **c**_____ that when I toss a coin, I get a head.

It is **d**_____ that it will be cold in February.

It is **e**_____ that Christmas Day this year is on 25th December.

Example

Shelley and Naznim are playing a game with spinners.

Shelley's   Naznim's
spinner   spinner

It is **f**_____ for Naznim to spin a six.

g_____ is more likely to spin a three, because she has **h**_____ threes.

If the winner is the girl with the highest score, then **i**_____ is the more likely to win because she has more higher numbers than Naznim.

10.2 Probability fractions LEVEL 5

When we have a situation giving us a number of equally likely events, then we can often give the event a probability in the form of a fraction. For example:

Answers can be found on page 56

Rolling a dice and getting a five has a probability of $\frac{1}{6}$ because there is only one way of getting a five, and six ways to get all the possible numbers.

Rolling a dice and getting an odd number has a probability of $\frac{3}{6}$ because there are three odd numbers and six possibilities. This will cancel down to $\frac{1}{2}$.

In a bag of sweets, 3 are toffees and 5 are mints:
The probability of taking out a toffee is $\frac{3}{8}$.
The probability of taking out a mint is **j**_____

Probability line

Probabilities can be shown on a probability line as here:

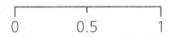

0   0.5   1

On the left is the probability of **impossible**, which is 0.
On the right is the probability of **certain**, which is 1.

Every other probability can be shown as a fraction between 0 and 1.
For example:

Harry has a spinner:

   A   The probability of spinning a four is **k**_____

   B   The probability of spinning a two is **l**_____

   C   The probability of spinning a six is **m**_____

   D   The probability of spinning an even number is **n**_____

   E   The probability of spinning an odd number is **o**_____

Each of these probabilities can be placed on the probability line, as shown here.

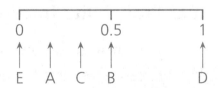

Answers can be found on page 56

Answers to self-check questions

Topic 1 Number

a tens
b hundreds
c right
d 000
e 86
f 88
g down to 760 (because of the 1)
h down to 300 (because of the 2)
i up to 9000 (because of the 5)
j up to 4 (because of the 5)
k up to 4.7 (because of the 7)
l units
m 27
n 24

o
$$\begin{array}{r} 23 \\ 17\overline{)391} \\ 34 \\ \hline 51 \end{array}$$

p
$$\begin{array}{r} 31 \\ 32\overline{)992} \\ 96 \\ \hline 32 \end{array}$$

q
$$\begin{array}{r} 37 \\ 26\overline{)962} \\ 78 \\ \hline 182 \end{array}$$

r 110 in each box
s 362 in each box

t
$$\begin{array}{r} 43 \qquad 43 \\ \times\ 39 \\ \hline 387 \\ 1290 \\ \hline 1677 \end{array}$$

u 34
$$\begin{array}{r} 26 \\ \times\ 34 \\ \hline 104 \\ 780 \\ \hline 884 \end{array}$$

Topic 2 Number Pattern

a 1, 3, 5, 7, 9, 11, 13, 15, 17, 19
b 2, 4, 6, 8, 10, 12, 14, 16, 18, 20
c $9 \times 9 = 81$
d 1, 4, 9, 16, 25, 36, 49, 64, 81, 100
e 1, 2, 3, 4, 6 and 12
f 5, 10, 15, 20, 25, etc.
g 13, 17, 19, 23, 29
h $10^3 = 1000$
i even
j threes
k 2
l $2°$
m $12°$
n $17°$
o $5°$
p $2°$
q -2
r -5
s -3

Topic 3 Fractions and percentages

a $\dfrac{2 \times 4}{5 \times 4}$
b $1\frac{19}{30}$
c 12
d 15
e 16 out of 100
f $\frac{27}{100}$
g £1.60
h 60%
i English (80%)

Topic 4 Symmetry

a one
b two
c three
d two
e 6
f 6

Topic 5 Co-ordinates

a (1, 4)
b (2, 1)

Topic 6 Shapes

a rectangle
b hexagon
c rectangle
d circle
e 3
f angles
g 2
h equal
i parallel
j D
k rotated
l translated
m edges
n cube
o sphere, cylinder
p pyramid
q $40°$
r $110°$
s $220°$
t $75°$
u $a = 130°, b = 50°$
v $a = 60°, b = c = d = 120°$
w outside
x 12 cm
y $6\,cm^2$
z $12\,cm^3$

Topic 7 Measures

a 40 mm, i.e. 4 cm
b millimetres
c metres
d kilometres
e 2.6 m
f 1.275 km
g less
h more
i less
j 1000
k smaller
l multiply
m divide
n less
o more
p less
q afternoon
r 19.00
s 11.00

Topic 8 Data handling

a Tom
b Vicky
c 5 cm
d Fatima
e 2
f jacket potato and
  baked beans
g 5
h 10
i 6
j 8
k 26
l 5
m 39°C
n frequency
o 86
p 3
q bus
r 50
s 25
t 25%

Topic 9 Averages

a blue
b 6
c 7.5 or $7\frac{1}{2}$
d adding
e 35
f 7
g 7
h mean

Topic 10 Probability

a impossible
b unlikely
c evens
d likely
e certain
f impossible
g Naznim
h 2
i Shelley
j $\frac{5}{8}$
k $\frac{1}{6}$
l $\frac{1}{2}$
m $\frac{1}{3}$
n 1
o 0

PART 2
Test practice papers

If you feel that, after working through Part 1, your child is ready, then try each of the two Test practice papers that you will find in this part of the book. One is for use *without a calculator* (Test A) and one is for use *with a calculator* (Test B), as in the National Tests themselves.

Taking the practice tests

Help your child to reconstruct the conditions that they will experience in the actual Tests.

- Find a place at home which is comfortable and reasonably quiet.
- Make sure that your child has two sharpened pencils.
- To time the Test, make sure that you set an alarm clock to go off after 45 minutes, but if your child does not finish in this time let them continue until they have. By timing the Test you will be able to assess how well your child is working in the time. It will also give your child a chance to see exactly how much time they will have in the National Test itself.

Mental arithmetic
A mental arithmetic test has been introduced for the first time in the National Tests in 1998.

Marking the questions

You should be responsible for marking your child's practice Test. You will find the answers and a breakdown of the marks awarded on pages 77–83. There are tips provided with the answers to help you to explain the answers to your child.

On page 84 you will find a **marking grid** to help you convert your child's marks into a *level* of performance.

Test A

Calculators not allowed (Time: 45 minutes)

Instructions

- Answer all the questions that you can in about 45 minutes.

- Make sure you do this paper without your calculator, use paper and pencil to do multiplication and division methods as well as your mental ability.

- Once you have finished, ask a parent to go to the answer section to see how many you got right.

- You will make mistakes – learn from them and build up your skills.

Tips before you start

- If you cannot answer a question – leave it – go on to the next question, and go back to the difficult question later.

- When you have finished go back and check your answers.

- Do read the instructions carefully, so that you are answering the question that has been asked.

- You cannot use your calculator in this paper, so do be ready for those questions where you need to calculate.

- If a question says calculate with the words 'show your working', then do show how you are calculating – it will gain you marks.

- If a question says 'explain', make sure you write your explanation in clear English.

Q1 Write the missing numbers in the boxes.

$$3 \times 30 = \boxed{}$$

$$\boxed{} + 57 = 75$$

$$80 - \boxed{} = 37$$

3
Q1

Answers can be found on page 77

Q2 In the box write $+$, $-$, $\times$ or $\div$ to make the calculation correct.

$6 \times 4 \boxed{} 7 = 17$

Q3 Joy and Kim go to the shops.

Doll	Football	Starship	Twister
£4.60	£2.50	£7.35	£3.50

a Kim has £5. He buys one thing from the shop and has £1.50 left.
What did he buy? . . . .

b Joy has £10 and buys the doll.
How much money has she **left**? . . . .

Q4 Tom uses a six-sided spinner.

Draw lines to show how **likely** the following are. An example is given.

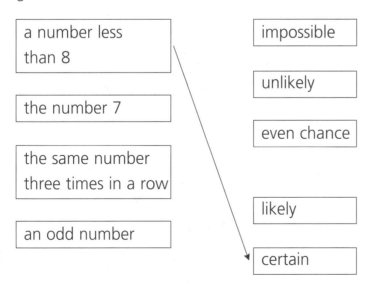

a number less than 8	impossible
the number 7	unlikely
the same number three times in a row	even chance
an odd number	likely
	certain

Answers can be found on page 77

Q5 Complete the table:

Shape	Property of shape		
	4 sides only	one or more right angles	two pairs of parallel sides
	✓	✓	✓

2

Q5

Q6 A number multiplied by itself gives the answer 36.
Circle the number.

2 3 4 5 6 7 8 9

1

Q6

Q7 Here are some shapes.

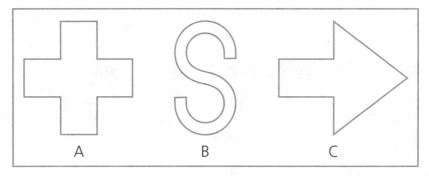

 A   B   C

a Put a tick (✓) in the box if the shape has reflective symmetry.

A ☐   B ☐   C ☐

2

Q7a

b Draw a line of symmetry
on this shape

1

Q7b

Answers can be found on page 77

Q8 Here are the times of some television programmes:

Channel 1	Channel 3	Channel 5
5.00 Sport	5.00 News	5.00 News
5.30 Cartoon	5.10 Sport	6.05 Historical drama
5.35 Film	5.20 Cartoon	6.55 Action drama
7.05 Comedy	5.50 Coastguards	7.50 Sport
7.45 Quiz show	6.40 Telly clips	8.10 Film
8.05 Crime drama	7.10 Film	10.40 Late show

a What is showing on **Channel 3** at **ten past six**?

. . . .

1
Q8a

b Chris watches the historical drama and then changes to
Channel 1 at the end.
What is showing on **Channel 1** when he changes channel?

. . . .

1
Q8b

c The film on **Channel 3** starts at **7.10**. It lasts for **one and a
half hours**.
At what time does the film end?

. . . .

1
Q8c

Q9 A line starts at *P* and goes
along the dotted lines to *Q*.
It divides the area of the
grid into **halves**.

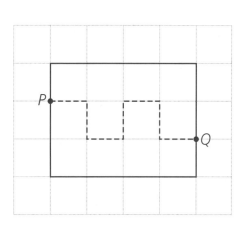

Answers can be found on page 78

Divide the area of the grid opposite into **halves**. Start at P and go to Q along the lines of the grid.

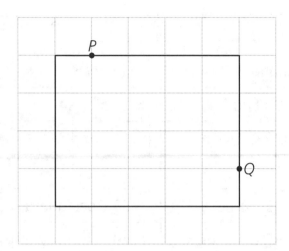

Q9

Q10 Write what the two missing **digits** could be.

$$\boxed{}\,7\,3\;+\;\boxed{}\,8\,4\;=\;657$$

Q10

Q11 Jesse puts **5 pegs** into a pegboard.

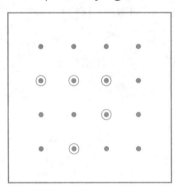 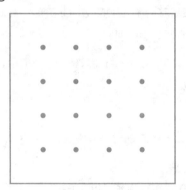

She turns the board through **1 right angle**.
Draw how the board looks now in the empty grid on the right above.

Q11

Q12 Here is a number sequence.

a Write the missing number.

1   2   4   7   11   16 $\boxed{}$

Q12a

b Explain how you worked it out.

. . . .

. . . .

. . . .

Q12b

Answers can be found on page 78

62

Q13 Here is a rectangle.

a   What are the co-ordinates of *D*?

(. . . . . , ...)

b   *T* is half way between *B* and *C*.
What are the co-ordinates of *T*?

(. . . . . , ...)

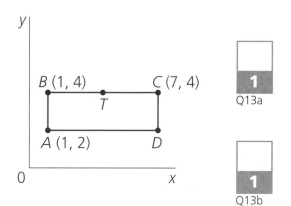

Q14 **Six** number dominoes are put into a bag.

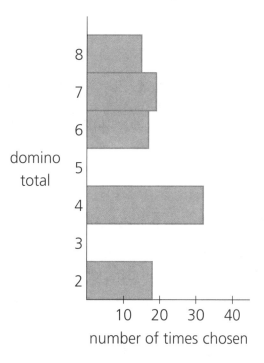

Ben takes one domino out and finds the total of the two numbers. He then puts the domino back into the bag.

He did this 100 times, and opposite is a graph of his results.

a   Give a reason why the **total 5 never** came up.

. . . .

. . . .

Answers can be found on page 79

b Give a reason why the **total 4** came up **most often**.

. . . .

. . . .

Q15 This diagram shows the proportions of money spent by a family on holiday.

ice cream and sweets
food
entertainment
accommodation

a Estimate what **fraction** of the money is spent on entertainment.

. . . .

b The family spent £320 on accommodation on this holiday.

Use the diagram to estimate **how much** was spent on ice creams and sweets.

. . . .

c The family spent £150 on food and 60% of this was spent on evening meals.
How much did they spend on evening meals?
(Show your working – it may earn you a mark.)

. . . .

Q16 Write in the missing digit.

$$\boxed{}\,7 \times 7 = 329$$

Answers can be found on page 79

Q17 This shape is made from rectangles and triangles. Each **rectangle** is the **same size** and each **triangle** is the **same size**. What is the **area** of the **whole shape**?

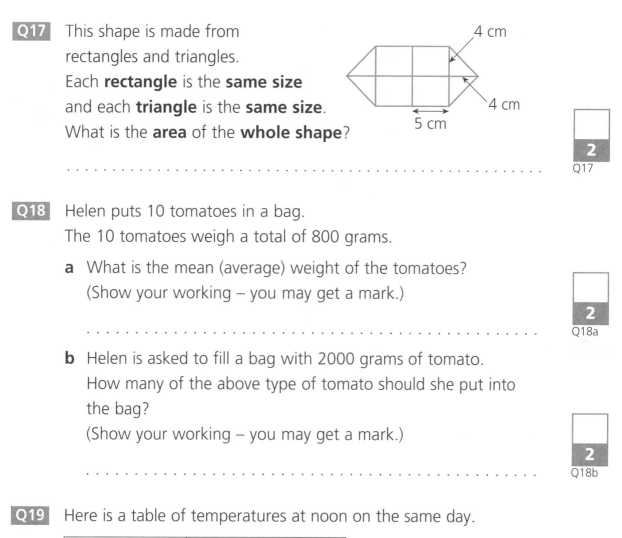

4 cm

4 cm

5 cm

. . . .

2 Q17

Q18 Helen puts 10 tomatoes in a bag.
The 10 tomatoes weigh a total of 800 grams.

a What is the mean (average) weight of the tomatoes?
(Show your working – you may get a mark.)

. . . .

2 Q18a

b Helen is asked to fill a bag with 2000 grams of tomato.
How many of the above type of tomato should she put into the bag?
(Show your working – you may get a mark.)

. . . .

2 Q18b

Q19 Here is a table of temperatures at noon on the same day.

City	Temperature (°C)
Newcastle	−4°C
Sheffield	−3°C
Birmingham	−1°C
London	2°C
Bristol	5°C

a What is the difference in temperature between London and Sheffield?

. . . .

1 Q19a

b By mid-afternoon, the temperature in Newcastle had risen by 3°C. What is the mid-afternoon temperature in Newcastle?

. . . .

1 Q19b

Answers can be found on page 79

Q20 A packet of crisps and a bottle of lemonade together cost 70 p.
Two packets of crisps and a bottle of lemonade together cost 95 p.

a What does a bottle of lemonade cost?

. . . .

b Explain how you got your answer.

. . . .

. . . .

. . . .

Q21 Here is a sketch of a triangle.

3 cm

4 cm

a Draw this triangle accurately, full size.

b Here is an accurately drawn triangle.

A

Use a protractor to measure the size of the angle marked *A*.

. . . .

Total = 43 marks

Answers can be found on page 79

Test B

Calculators allowed (Time: 45 minutes)

Instructions

- Answer all the questions that you can in about 45 minutes.

- You can use your calculator, so make sure you do use it where you need to.

- Once you have finished, ask a parent to go to the answer section to see how many you got right.

- You will make mistakes – learn from them and build up your skills.

Tips before you start

- If you cannot answer a question – leave it – go on to the next question, and go back to the difficult question later.

- When you have finished, go back through your answers and check what you have done.

- Do read the instructions carefully, so that you are answering the question that has been asked.

- If a question says 'calculate', then it expects you to use your calculator.

- If a question says 'explain', make sure you write your explanation in clear English.

Q1 **a** Write what the three missing numbers could be.

$$\boxed{} + \boxed{} + \boxed{} = 64$$

1
Q1a

b Write what the two missing numbers could be.

$$70 - \boxed{} - \boxed{} = 45$$

1
Q1b

Answers can be found on page 80

Q2 Clive arrives at the car park with these coins in his pocket.

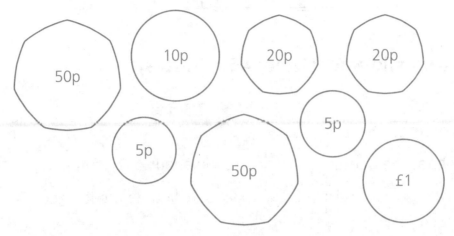

a How much has he in his pocket?

. . . .

1

Q2a

b He must put the **exact** amount of 85 p into a ticket machine. Which of the coins must he put in?

. . . .

1

Q2b

Q3 Kerry did a survey on the types of vehicle that arrived at her school between 10 am and 2 pm

	Number of vehicles arriving at school ⊥⊥⊦⊤ *stands for 5 vehicles*
Cars	⊥⊦⊦⊤ IIII
Vans	⊥⊦⊦⊤ I
Lorries	III
Taxis	II

a How many vehicles arrived at Kerry's school during this survey?

. . . .

1

Q3a

b How many **more cars** arrived than **lorries**?

1

Q3b

. . . .

Answers can be found on page 80

c Here is part of a bar chart of the information.
Draw the **two** missing bars.

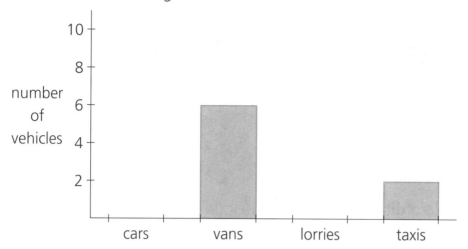

Q3c

Q4 Here are two calculations with some signs missing.
Write in the correct **signs**.

a $5 \times 2 \times 3 \boxed{} 5 = 25$

Q4a

b $5 \boxed{} 3 \boxed{} 2 \boxed{} 4 = 7$

Q4b

Q5 Write what the missing numbers could be.

a $\boxed{}$ is an even number greater that 18.

Q5a

b $\boxed{}$ is a number greater than 70 and can be divided
by 3 with no remainder.

Q5b

Q6 Miss Terry took all her class of **28** pupils to a theme park.
It cost **£3.25** for each pupil to go into the theme park.
Miss Terry got in for free.

a How much did Miss Terry have to pay altogether for all the
class to go into the theme park?

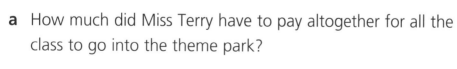

Q6a

b Miss Terry had **£10** left.
She saw that ice creams were **35p** each.
Could she afford to buy all her pupils an ice cream? . . . .

Q6b

Answers can be found on page 80

Q7 Andrew has drawn a shape on this grid.

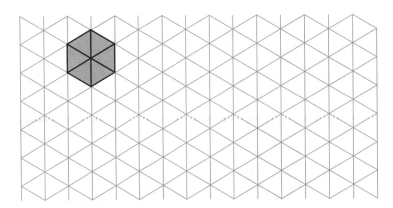

a Draw a **different** shape on the grid that has the **same area** as Andrew's shape.
  Label this shape 'same'.

Q7a

b Draw a shape on the grid that has an area **smaller** than Andrew's shape.
  Label this shape 'smaller'.

Q7b

Q8 a An apple that weighs 300 grams is placed on a set of scales.

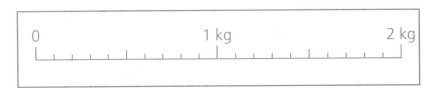

Mark an **arrow** (↓) on the scales to show the reading for **300 g**.

Q8a

b A bag of apples was placed on the scales.
  The scales showed the weight as:

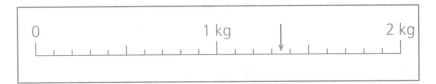

What is the **total weight** of these apples?

Q8b

. . . .

Answers can be found on page 80

Q9 This is a cube.

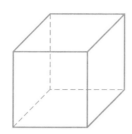

Put a tick (✓) for each diagram **if it is a net** for a cube.
Put a cross (✗) if it is not.

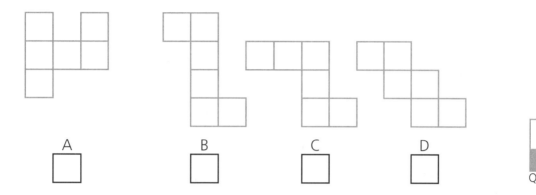

A ☐ B ☐ C ☐ D ☐

2
Q9

Q10 **a** The rule for this number sequence is

'double and add 1'

Write in the missing number.

1 ⟶ 3 ⟶ 7 ⟶ 15 ⟶ ☐

1
Q10a

b Here is part of another sequence with the same rule.
Write in the missing number.

☐ ⟶ 9 ⟶ 19 ⟶ 39

1
Q10b

Q11 Use a ruler to draw 2 more lines to make an **isosceles** triangle.

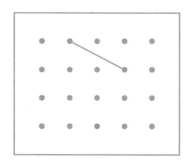

1
Q11

Answers can be found on page 81

Q12 This table shows the distances in miles between five towns.

	Cam.	Hull	Liv.	Shef.	Lon.
Cambridge		140	193	123	60
Hull	140		129	66	188
Liverpool	193	129		80	216
Sheffield	123	66	80		168
London	60	188	216	168	

a Use the table to find the distance from **Liverpool** to **Hull**.

. . . .

1
Q12a

b Peter goes from **London** to **Sheffield** and then on to
Cambridge. How many **miles** does he travel?
(Show your method – you may get a mark.)

. . . .

2
Q12b

Q13 The weather in April always changes from cool to warm.

a Look at this temperature chart for middays in April one year.

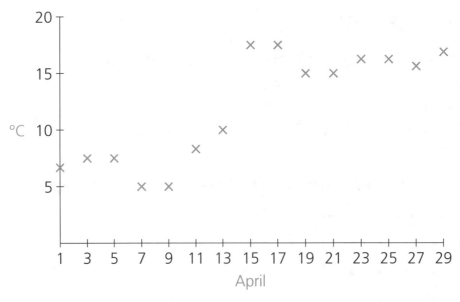

When did the midday temperature first reach 10°C?

. . . .

1
Q13a

Answers can be found on page 81

b Which dates showed the largest midday temperature change from one recorded date to the next?

. . . .

c Estimate what the midday temperature was on 22nd April.

. . . .

Q14 Complete this three-digit number so that it is a **multiple of 9**.

4		

Q15 At the greengrocer's there is a scale for converting pounds weight and kilograms.

pounds weight

0   10   20

kilograms

a Approximately how many kilograms are there in 5 pounds weight?

. . . .

b Approximately how many pounds weight are there in 8 kilograms?
Give your answer to 1 decimal place. . . . .

Q16 Sita thinks of a number. She divides it by **11**. Her answer is **72**.

What is the number that Sita thinks of? . . . .

Q17 Fill in the empty boxes to complete the pattern.

$n + 5$		$9n + 5$
	$5n + 3$	$9n + 3$
n	$5n$	

Answers can be found on page 81

Q18 Here are some numbers:

3   5   7   11

a Use **two** of these numbers to make a
fraction which is greater than $\frac{1}{2}$, but less than 1.

1 Q18a

b What **fraction** must you **add** to the fraction to make it **1**?

. . . .

1 Q18b

Q19 **a** Draw the **reflection** of the shape below in the mirror line.

2 Q19a

b The shape on the grid below is rotated 180° about the point C.
Draw the shape in its new position.

2 Q19b

Q20 Bernie planted tulip bulbs in his garden. He used 2 yellow tulips
to every 3 red tulips. He used 105 bulbs altogether.

How many yellow tulips did he use?
(Show your method – you may get a mark.)

. . . .

2 Q20

Total = 43 marks

Answers can be found on page 82

Mental Arithmetic Test

Instructions

- Ask one of your parents or an elder brother or sister or a Granny to help, in fact anyone older than you who can read the questions confidently!

- Ask them to read each question to you *twice*, then to give you ten seconds to write down the answer.

- If you use your own paper to write the answers on, you can use this same mental test more than once to help you.

- You must *not* use a calculator.

- You must *not* write down any calculation, it must all happen in your head – only the *answer* must be written down.

- **Read each question twice, clearly and slowly.**

- **Allow 10 seconds for each question to be answered.**

Q1 Write, in figures, the number four thousand and twenty three.

Q2 What number should you subtract from twenty to get the answer twelve?

Q3 What is thirty-two multiplied by ten?

Q4 In a class, one-half of the class is boys. What percentage of the class is girls?

Q5 What is twenty-four divided by eight?

Q6 Change one hundred and thirty millimetres into centimetres.

Q7 What is forty-three doubled?

Q8 What is twenty-five multiplied by one hundred?

Answers can be found on page 83

Q9 How many five pences make thirty-five pence?

Q10 What is £5.60 to the nearest pound?

Q11 What number is halfway between fifteen and twenty-one?

Q12 A television programme starts at a quarter to six. It lasts twenty minutes.
At what time does the programme finish?

Q13 One-third of a number is fifteen. What is the number?

Q14 A bag contains £5, all in ten pence pieces. How many coins are there in the bag?

Q15 What number is six squared?

Q16 Subtract nineteen from sixty-five.

Q17 Glasgow was minus four degrees; Southampton was five degrees.
How much colder was Glasgow than Southampton?

Q18 What is ten per cent of £85?

Q19 What is one-quarter of thirty-six?

Q20 Add together one-and-a-half metres and fifty centimetres.

Answers can be found on page 83

Answers: Test A

Q1 The missing numbers are 90, 18 and 43   `3`

Q2 The missing sign is a minus, −   `1`

Q3 **a** Kim bought a Twister   **b** Joy had £5.40 left   `2`

Q4 The lines should go as shown:

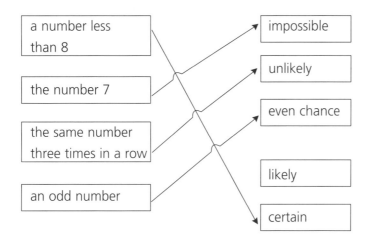

You will gain 2 marks for all lines correct, and 1 mark if you have two correct.   `2`

Q5 You should have the two rows completed as;

▱	✓	✗	✓
⊔	✗	✓	✗

You will gain 2 marks if you have no errors, and 1 mark if you have only 1 or 2 errors.   `2`

Q6 The number 6 should be circled.   `1`

Q7 **a** You should have ticked A and C, gaining 2 marks if it is all correct, and 1 mark if you only made 1 error.

      b You should have drawn in one of the lines dotted as shown opposite.

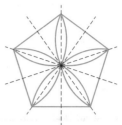

`2`

`1`

Q8 **a** 'Coastguards' is showing on Channel 3 at ten past six.

      b After switching to Channel 1 he will be watching the end of the film.

      c The Channel 3 film ends at 8.40.

`1`

`1`

`1`

Q9 There are a lot of different correct answers to this question, such as:

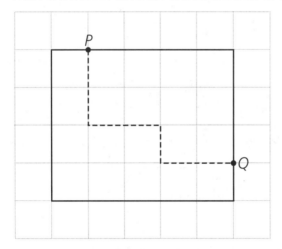

As long as your line divides each part into 10 squares, it should be correct.

`1`

Q10 Because the 73 and the 84 add up to 157, the hundreds just have to add up to 5 to give a total of 657.

So the two numbers that you put in must add up to 5

`1`

Q11 You could end up with either of the following diagrams, the difference between them is that one has gone clockwise, the other anticlockwise.

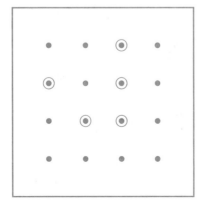 *or* 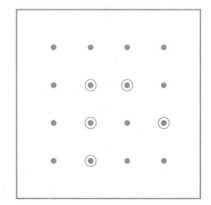

`1`

Q12 a 22 is the next number. `1`

  b It is found by looking at the differences between successive terms, i.e. 1, 2, 3, 4 and 5, so the next difference has to be 6, which when added to 16, gives us 22. `1`

Q13 a D is (7, 2)   **b** T is (4, 4) `2`

Q14 a Total 5 never came up because there was no combination of numbers on the dominoes Ben has that gives a total of 5. `1`

  b The total 4 came up most often because there are more ways of getting a four than any other number. There are two ways to get a four. `1`

Q15 a Entertainment is about $\frac{1}{4}$ of the money. You would get a mark if your fraction was between $\frac{1}{5}$ and $\frac{1}{3}$, or between 0.2 and 0.3. `1`

  b You should see that the amount spent on ice cream and sweets is one-quarter of the amount spent on accommodation. So the amount we are looking for is: £320 ÷ 4 = £80. You would still earn your mark for an answer between £70 and £90. `1`

  c 60% of £150 = 150 × 60 ÷ 100 = £90 `2`

Q16 329 ÷ 7 = 47. So the missing digit is 4. `1`

Q17 Each rectangle area = 4 × 5 = 20 cm²
Each triangle area = $\frac{1}{2}$ × 4 × 4 = 8 cm²
Total area = (4 × 20) + (4 × 8) = 112 cm² `2`

Q18 a Mean = 800 ÷ 10 = 80 g `2`

  b You need to calculate 2000 ÷ 80 = 25 tomatoes. `2`

Q19 a Between London and Sheffield there is 5°C. `1`

  b Mid-afternoon temperature in Newcastle is −4 + 3 = −1°C. `1`

Q20 a A bottle of lemonade is 45 p. `1`

  b Subtract the cost of a bottle and a packet of crisps from 2 packets of crisps and 1 bottle. This will give us the price of one packet of crisps at 25 p. We now just subtract the 25 p from the cost of crisps and bottle to give us the price of 45 p. `1`

Q21 a If your diagram is correct, angles no more than 2° out and the lines no more than 1 mm out, then you will earn 1 mark. `1`

  b The angle should be measured at 35°. (You still get the mark for 33° to 37°.) `1`

Total = 43 marks

Answers: Test B

Q1 **a** There are hundreds of different correct answers, as long as your answers add up to 64, you will gain the mark.

b Your two numbers need to add up to 25.

Q2 **a** £2.60

b 85 p can be made exactly with the 50 p, 20 p, 10 p and a 5 p

Q3 **a** 20 vehicles came altogether.

b There were 6 more cars than lorries.

c Your completed diagram should look like this.

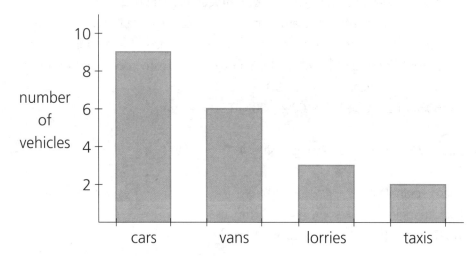

Q4 **a** − (minus sign) **b** $5 \times 3 - 2 \times 4$ or $5 + 3 \times 2 - 4$

Q5 **a** Any even number over 18 will do, e.g. 20, 22, 24, 26, etc.

b The number must be bigger than 70, and the digits must add up to a multiple of 3, e.g. 72, 75, 78, 81, etc.

Q6 **a** $28 \times £3.25 = £91$

b $28 \times 35\,p = £9.80$, yes she can buy them all an ice cream.

Q7 **a** There are many different, correct answers, they all use 6 triangles.

b Any shape with an area less than 6 of these little triangles.

Q8 **a** The answer should look like the figure below.

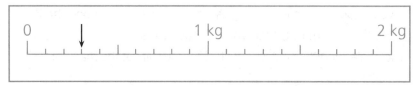

b The total weight of the apples is 1350 g or 1.35 kg.

80

Q9 There should be a tick next to B and D, with a cross next to A and C.
Score 2 marks with no errors, and 1 mark with just 1 error.

`2`

Q10 a 31 **b** 4

`2`

Q11 There are a number of correct possible answers, two of the most common answers are:

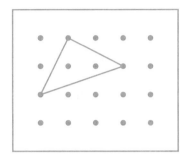 *or*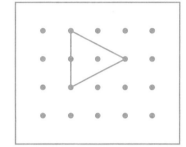

`1`

Q12 a Liverpool to Hull is 129 miles.

`1`

b London to Sheffield is 168 miles, then on to Cambridge, a further 123 miles.
This gives a total of $168 + 123 = 291$ miles.

`2`

Q13 a Temperature first reaches 10°C on April 13th.

`1`

b The largest midday temperature change is from 13th April to 15th April.

`1`

c The midday temperature on 22nd April is estimated at halfway between the temperature on 21st and 23rd April, this is 16°C.

`1`

Q14 There are a lot of different correct answers, as long as all the digits add up to a multiple of 9, then the number itself is a multiple of 9. For example 450, 414, 495 etc.

`1`

Q15 a 2.5 kg is approximately equivalent to 5 pounds weight.

`1`

b 8 kg is equivalent to 17.6 pounds weight. An answer between 17.1 and 17.9 will gain the mark.

`1`

Q16 $11 \times 72 = 792$

`1`

Q17 The boxes should be filled in as

	$5n + 5$	
$n + 3$		
		$9n$

You gain 2 marks if it is all correct, and 1 mark for only one error.

`2`

Q18 **a** You could have $\frac{3}{5}$ or $\frac{5}{7}$ or $\frac{7}{11}$

b From $\frac{3}{5}$ you would have to add $\frac{2}{5}$

From $\frac{5}{7}$ you would have to add $\frac{2}{7}$

From $\frac{7}{11}$ you would have to add $\frac{4}{11}$

Q19 **a** 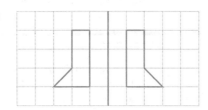 **b**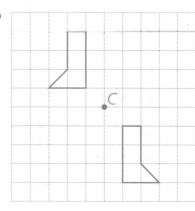

Q20 $105 \div (2 + 3) = 21$

He would use 21×2 yellow tulips which is 42.

Total = 43 marks

Answers: Mental Arithmetic Test

There is one mark for each question.
Do not award a mark if any marking has been made on paper.

Q1	4023		**Q11**	18
Q2	8		**Q12**	5 past 6 or 6.05
Q3	320		**Q13**	45
Q4	50		**Q14**	50
Q5	3		**Q15**	36
Q6	13		**Q16**	46
Q7	86		**Q17**	9 degrees
Q8	2500		**Q18**	£8.50
Q9	7		**Q19**	9
Q10	6		**Q20**	2 metres or 200 centimetres

Marking grid

Test A: no calculator (pages 58–66)

Question	Marks available	Marks scored
1	3	
2	1	
3	2	
4	2	
5	2	
6	1	
7	3	
8	3	
9	1	
10	1	
11	1	
12	2	
13	2	
14	2	
15	4	
16	1	
17	2	
18	4	
19	2	
20	2	
21	2	
total	**43**	

Test B: calculator (pages 67–74)

Marks available	Marks scored
2	
2	
4	
2	
2	
2	
2	
2	
2	
2	
1	
3	
3	
1	
2	
1	
2	
2	
4	
2	
43	

Mental Arithmetic Test (pages 75–76)

Marks available	Marks scored
1	
1	
1	
1	
1	
1	
1	
1	
1	
1	
1	
1	
1	
1	
1	
1	
1	
1	
1	
1	
20	

Using the marking grid

	Test A	Test B	Mental test	Test A + B + Mental
Maximum mark	43	43	20	106
Level 3	10–22	10–22	7–11	27–55
Level 4	23–33	23–33	12–16	56–82
Level 5	34–43	34–43	17–20	83–106

Mark scored in Test A [ ] ▶ Level [ ]

Mark scored in Test B [ ] ▶ Level [ ]

Mark scored in Mental Arithmetic Test [ ] ▶ Level [ ]

Total [ ] ▶ Level [ ]